HOW TO HAVE A GREAT INTERNATIONAL WEDDING
Without Robbing A Bank

BY

Sandy L. Brown

authorHOUSE®

AuthorHouse™
1663 Liberty Drive
Bloomington, IN 47403
www.authorhouse.com
Phone: 1-800-839-8640

First published by AuthorHouse 9/9/2009

ISBN: 978-1-4389-7607-5 (e)
ISBN: 978-1-4389-7606-8 (sc)

Library of Congress Control Number: 2009906778

Printed in the United States of America
Bloomington, Indiana

This book is printed on acid-free paper.

INTRODUCTION

I did it again! I got married for the second time and it is wonderful, even though I believed for years that my first attempt was enough. This book exists because I found an amazing man after many years of being divorced. My new husband and I wanted to do things differently since this is the second marriage for both of us.

This book fits all marital situations, whether it is your first marriage or the fourth marriage; whether you are getting married in the Bahamas (like us) or in Europe; whether you are a young couple or an older couple or despite if you are "well -to- do" financially or have a modest income. There will be "something" in this book that you can take from and make it your own.

ACKNOWLEDGEMENTS

This book is in memory of my late girlfriend, Yvonne, who triumphantly made it from California to the Bahamas with end stage cancer just to be a part of our wedding. This book is also dedicated to our family and close friends who attended our wedding and shared in our lovely beginning. Additionally, this book is also dedicated to any of you who want to celebrate your love by having a "non-traditional" different type of wedding that you and your guests will never, ever forget!

A special thank you to my brother David whose love gives me strength, my brother Steve, my sisters-in-law Shonda and Agnes, Grandma , my good sister-friends Charisse, Linda, Jeanette and Hazel, along with Jeff, Roberta and their families, who usually support my projects.

Edited by Claire Joseph, Masters in both English and Library Science

- Some names may have been changed by request.

TABLE OF CONTENTS

CHAPTER 1
THE INITIAL PLANNING STAGE
and WHAT TO CONSIDER

The love that my husband Jason and I share is very comfortable and has "no traffic" which is my husband`s way of saying that our marriage is peaceful and calm. This is the second marriage for both of us and we wanted to do it in a very uniquely, exciting and special way. Our first consideration was to decide our wedding date. It was of the utmost importance that we did not choose a month in which either of us had previously wed in. We were therefore comfortably able to exclude August and December.

Another consideration to ponder is the kind of weather or type of climate one prefers for not only the wedding but also for your honeymoon. Sometimes the honeymoon needs become seriously diminished by the preciseness of the wedding detail, however, when you are preparing for an unconventional wedding, you want to bring the honeymoon to the forefront.

One of the win-win realities for me in considering a Caribbean wedding was that the honeymoon could start right away! I recall thinking: how great is that! My first marriage`s honeymoon took place many years ago in the Poconos, Pennsylvania at the "Mount Airy Lodge" (now known as Mount Airy Casino Resort). I stayed up all night tediously packing for us both after the wedding reception followed by the additional party at my parents home, (while my new husband slept). We also had to say good-bye to some of the out-of-state relatives since we were driving to the Poconos from New York early in the morning. The long drive from Long Island to Mount Airy Lodge was the second thing to usurp wind out of the sails of love! Trust me when I tell you that you do not want "anything" to take positive energy from your very special occasion: the honeymoon.

Jason and I went online to research "international weddings" and found that many domestic and Caribbean resorts have promotions that offer wedding packages if you reside with them from as few as 24 hours through up to

75 hours, depending upon the location of the resort or country. These packages vary from quite expensive to very reasonable, depending on your taste and desires. You **will** find exactly what you and your spouse-to-be are looking for all over the world. A few years ago my co-worker`s brother got married in a beautiful large castle in Florida. The reception was included with the rental of the lovely, spacious castle which was housed on a well manicured landscape. The Castle, where there was room service and the usual hotel amenities, was the destination for all of the relatives and other guests of this bride and groom to further enjoy this "fairy tale-like" event. The pictures of this wedding were absolutely breath-taking along with the vast acreage of land. The family and friends who attended this awesome wedding had a "priceless" experience that is not likely to be forgotten. This is a good example of a non-traditional wedding that occurred right here in the United States.

Years ago while on vacation, I stayed at the Holiday Inn Resort in Montego Bay, Jamaica W.I. Being born and raised in New York, I felt certain that I was quite familiar with "Holiday Inns" everywhere, however, they had nothing in common with this one except the name. The main lobby area is completely open on all sides with beautiful tropical plants everywhere and flowers adorning the registration desk. The area that is the back of the lobby is also opened giving you a panoramic view of the pools, beach and ocean. It is like stepping into a movie or high tech video. The staff is very accommodating and brightly dressed in decorative uniforms. I found that this Resort offered a wedding package which included the Justice of the Peace, taped wedding music, a photographer, a small floral bouquet for the bride along with a boutonniere for the groom.

Dinner for the bride and groom with 2-4 guests followed immediately after the ceremony. During my stay I saw a few weddings, either in the garden or others in a gazebo near the ocean. In two cases the brides were dressed in beautiful white gowns that you would see in a traditional wedding. In the third wedding, the bride was more appropriately dressed for the hot tropical climate in a backless, sleeveless gown that was waltz length only in the back. She looked wonderful and was a great match for her groom who had on a white tuxedo jacket with matching white shorts. This couple really allowed the West Indian tropical culture drive their attire. Immediately, their union consisted of fun and synergism to match their love. Two hours later, I saw them in their bathing suits on the beach.

Jason and I decided that we would get married in the Bahamas at the Sandals Royal Bahamian Resort and Spa on Cable Beach. One of the reasons why we chose Sandals is because they offered three various packages for a wedding and a "wedding coordinator". Yes, you read it right! I had my own wedding coordinator from months before the wedding right up to the day of our ceremony. I was able to share ideas and get her opinion multiple times from Sandals 800 number in Miami prior to arriving in the Bahamas. Once at the Resort, the wedding coordinator on the premises knew all that had been arranged and then "pumped it up a notch" accenting the wedding day and wedding night. (You can believe that this time my wedding night was full of gusto and great energy.) She also coordinated the necessary paper work that had to be presented to the Magistrate by all couples wanting to marry prior to receiving permission to wed. Some of the paper-work required bringing our "original" documents from home.

The wedding coordinator also offered various little, let`s call them "aphrodisiac activities", that could be arranged for the wedding night, which

I will leave as a surprise. I will tell you that one of the offers I took advantage of was for one of the local beauticians to come to my room two hours before the wedding and style my hair. She did a magnificent job.

CHAPTER 2
PLANNING WHEN and WHERE

When it came time to choose our wedding date, our first consideration was to omit the months in which our first weddings occurred. We then looked at the time of year both of us liked and came up with the beginning of September because in New York the weather is between summer heat and the coolness of the beginning of Fall. It is important to consider the weather in your home town because when flying to your honeymoon destination you want to make sure that weather conditions are conducive to safe air travel and avoid snow conditions, for instance, that could delay departure and/or returns.

Now we have the place and month so picking the day is easy. We both wanted to get married on a Saturday or Sunday afternoon towards the beginning of the month. Looking at the calendar we realized that on or around Labor Day would be fine. We also felt that our family and friends might find it easier to be away for a long weekend if it encompassed a holiday.

I happily called my wedding coordinator and told her our preferred date and preference for Sunday. We found that the Bahamas does not permit internationals to wed on Sunday, so the date was set for Saturday, September 7th. There were options for where on the premises a couple could marry such as in the Garden, in the Garden Gazebo or in the Angelic Gazebo that is overlooking the ocean. Another beautiful area is the small island right across the ocean from Sandals beach and a boat ride away in a tropical open restaurant, bright with red, orange and lavender colors. This property was with a small private beach, two Jacuzzi's and a pool. This area would have been nice, in our view, for a less formal wedding where everyone could attend in their shorts and bathing suits and follow the ceremony with a swim. I knew I wanted to get married while overlooking the ocean with the blue water as the background. The actual choice was made when the wedding coordinator showed us the areas to choose from right after we arrived in the Bahamas.

We chose the location at the beginning of the ocean on a small balcony area that was approximately six feet above the ocean. This was in a white gazebo adorned with angels around the opened top, so that the ocean breeze could blow on us with the beautiful blue water behind us. It was like a movie setting that could not have been made by man.

There was a long red carpet leading from the walkway across the sand to the gazebo just for the wedding party, as well as the guests to walk on. Chairs were placed to the right and left of this carpet for our family and friends. The view alone brought tears to the eyes of both the male and female guests. Many of the other hotel guests waved and applauded as the hotel staff escorted me in my wedding gown, past two pool areas to the red carpet. Others followed me and watched as Jason; standing next to the minister, awaited my march to the surreal altar. I felt like royalty and by the time I reached Jason I saw tears gently glistening his cheeks.

CHAPTER 3
HOW TO INVITE GUESTS IN A TIMELY MANNER

In recognizing the delicate functioning of most jobs regarding requesting time off, (if you are fortunate enough to have a job) we knew we had to let our family and friends know in advance of the expected six to eight week notification as is indicated for most weddings. We decided to make our own invitations utilizing an inexpensive wedding invitation program and beautiful floral stationary both found at my local Staples Office Supplies Store.

This is a good time to create a planning schedule. You will find that this schedule will help you to be more organized. A copy of the one we used is on the following page.

PLANNING SCHEDULE

6 Month

Know wedding & honeymoon thoughts

Get Passports for travel abroad

Have attendants choose dresses

Complete guest list

Order wedding rings

Check on possible hotels for guests

1 Month

Make final count of attendees

Send a card or paper note to guests

    inviting them to a "meet & greet"

in other country

5 Months

Mail invitations with detailed information

Order announcement ribbon and favors

Put in or apply for time off from job

3 Months

Buy attendants' gifts

Have gown fitting

Make home made favors (if not purchased)

2 Months

Send reminder cards to guests

Final dress fitting

We collectively decided what would be written and personally designed in the best way for us. The invitation letter was sent to approximately 65 people in March conveying our intent to marry in September at the Sandals Royal Bahamian Resort and Spa in the Bahamas. We wanted to send our guests all of the information they might need in deciding a place to stay in the Bahamas so that they did not have to look anything up unless they wanted to be away from the others. We sent information about the various packages at the Sandals Royal Bahamian Resort and Spa in case other couples wanted an all inclusive there. This information also included the Nassau Marriott Resort and Casino, (which was the name at that time) in Nassau and ten minutes away from the Sandals Resort. Of course, our guests could stay anywhere they chose to in Nassau, Cable Beach or Paradise Island; however, we just wanted to offer two areas in our letter.

Our travel agent at the time was of great help and assisted me in working out traveling deals for those who would like to stay at Sandals and for those who would prefer a more economic package. We offered the utilization of this travel agency to our invited guests although it was up to them to accept or use their own travel agency. Surprisingly, almost everyone who attended our wedding utilized our agent but, very wisely, Jason and I did not intervene between the guests and the travel agent when it came to handling their money.

We thought only about 10 to 12 people would attend, although we sent out 65 invitations. Jason did not have many friends at that time but he had a lot of "work-buddies" with whom he was quite social. Unfortunately, none of them were able to attend the wedding. His best man and usher was the husband of my matron-of-honor, Charisse. In August we sent all potential guests a reminder about the September wedding and to let them know that we were looking forward to seeing them. I was totally amazed that 45 people came to our wedding, among them were Jason`s two sisters and three cousins. Another good thing about having your wedding in another country is that you know the 200 to 250 wedding guests that you might feel obligated to invite if your wedding was at home, you cannot possibly invite to a wedding that is abroad.

Jason and I flew to the Bahamas on a major airline and I carried my gown in the special plastic garment bag specifically for wedding gowns. The stewardess for the first class section hung it up for me, as I preceded to my coach seat. The other stewardess gave the "in case you do not make it while in route instructions" of which neither Jason nor I could comprehend due to extreme happiness. Shortly into the flight a stewardess came to us and asked if we were getting married in the Bahamas, to which we both replied in unison, yes! She then told us to get our belongings and follow her. We complied and followed her into the first class section where she had our two seats waiting, along with two glasses of champagne. She wished us well on behalf of the airlines.

Having our wedding in a different country really made both of us feel like this was the first time marriage. It also was a bonus point for me that by law, we had to reside in the Bahamas at least 3 days prior to the marriage which helped to prompt the feeling of being an islander prior to our wedding day.

The beautiful blue ocean matched the sky while we were standing at the waters edge under a white gazebo with sculpted angels playing flutes on our wedding day. The site was so angelic that my emotions were overflowing. Jason is very even tempered and usually does not allow anything or anyone to shake him, however, he also cried.

CHAPTER 4
WEDDING DAY FAVORS and GUESTS GIFTS

Jason and I gave great thought to the unique gift that we wanted our guests to have. Since we are forty-something and a more mature age group than the usual first time bride and groom, we wanted the favors to be something that could be commemorative and utilized. We discussed our thoughts with my matron-of-honor, Charisse and her husband, James before reaching what we thought was a great idea. We decided to make a "lover`s music CD" consisting of songs that we liked throughout the years. Our groomsman, who had been making musical CDs for many years for his listening pleasure at home, burned the CDs for us after we decided on 12 great love songs by different artists. I found a label maker software package for under $15.00, therefore, I was able to easily make personalized labels for every CD.

We made more than we needed for the wedding day because Jason and I wanted to also give them to others who sent wedding gifts to us in lieu of attending. We had a total of 50 CDs to pack for the trip to the Bahamas.

I was feeling so good about our international wedding that I wanted to do something special for our guests who predominantly stayed at the Nassau Marriott Resort and Casino, as a thank you for deciding to spend their vacation time with us. I decided that I wanted to have a special little bag in their rooms upon their arrival to the hotel.

Therefore, Jason and I enlisted the help of a local cab driver who drove us downtown to a wholesale liquor store on the island to purchase bottles of champagne that we placed in small bags brought from home. In addition to champagne, we placed 2 fluted champagne glasses that had a ribbon with both our names, along with the wedding date around them. I had a box shipped of the glasses with ribbons already tied and packed from a UPS (United Parcel Service) store to Sandals Royal Bahamian Resort and Spa which saved us from trying to bring it along with luggage on the plane.

Having the small gift bags placed in our guests rooms was relatively easy to do by speaking with the management staff the day prior to their arrival. The hotel had their Bellmen handle placing the bags in the appropriate rooms as requested. Some hotels will do this for free and others have a fee for making this delivery. Needless to say, our guests thought this was great and added to what they had already considered to be an awesome occasion.

At Sandals, there is a daily fee for guests to come on premises and it is called a "pass". Jason and I had arranged for passes on our wedding day but we thought that it would be great for everyone to meet each other, as well as, to see us prior to the wedding. There is a Sports Bar in the casino area of the Marriott and so we had all guests, including the 4 couples that stayed at the Sandals Royal Resort, meet in that Sports Bar at 5:00pm the day before the wedding. The meeting notice was placed in everyone`s little gift bag, however, certainly attending would be by choice and independent of what we were financing on the wedding day. Surprisingly, most of our guests had met each other on the plane coming to the wedding. This was also a good time for my friends and family from out of state, to meet and talk with my husband-to-be. You can believe that we all had a great time.

Personalizing your plans are also a great activity

for both the bride and groom because the plans impact both families and invited guests. You will have a shared victory when you add your own touch, leaving your loved ones to ponder how your creativity escaped them.

CHAPTER 5
FINANCIAL ASPECTS

I am sure that you have been wondering if a wedding in the Bahamas or somewhere else may be out of your price range! The truth of the matter is, in my view, it is less expensive than one that Jason and I would have had at home with a guest list of at least 250 people. Our wedding was what we could comfortably handle financially, in addition it was absolutely beautiful. There were of course opportunities to spend more money, for example have the Sandals Royal Bahamian Resort band play for the reception instead of the DJ or to pay for all invited couples to stay at Sandals or pay for more flowers to adorn the gazebo that we married under, etc.

There are costs other than the bridal gown and tuxedo, of course. However, before I list some of the other costs, this is a good time to talk about the tuxedo for the groom. It is imperative that once the tuxedo is selected, the appropriate terms of the tuxedo rental must be discussed. This is important because the groom should arrange terms that are extensive enough to get through the length of the honeymoon to avoid penalty costs. Now, these can be some of the costs:

- All inclusive Sandals Resort package which includes air, transfers to and from the airport

- A day pass for all invited guests who are staying elsewhere (the pass includes food, drink and activities with use of the grounds)

- Bouquets for bridesmaids and boutonnieres for best men(the brides bouquet is frequently part of the package)

- Cost for wedding invitation software and special floral paper (you may use whatever paper suits you, however festive paper looks best)

- Purchase label maker for CDs

- Cost of having favors such as plastic champagne glasses packaged and shipped out a couple of weeks before the wedding (In our case the wedding coordinator in the Bahamas accepted the package)

- Cost of 30 bottles of Champagne

- Cost to have hotel place a gift bag in every guest room

- Photographer for pictures and/or video

You should do a little research and find out if there is a fee to enter or exit the country where you would like to marry. In the Bahamas there is an exit fee that is currently $15.00; therefore, you need to make sure that you have that money set aside. Also keep in mind that in other countries, weddings are handled differently than what we are accustomed to in the United States, thus I sent some of the things I wanted to have for my guests and as favors, ahead of time. I would have had a hard time finding, for instance, enough elegant fluted plastic champagne glasses within budget range for us. They would have had to use the glasses in their rooms or try to get room service to send them up which would have interfered with some of the loving "ambiance" I was trying to create.

Jason and I had the option of choosing from 3 different wedding packages at Sandals Resort. The highest of which, at the time Jason and I were there, involved a Rolls Royce to pick us up from the airport and to be at our disposal throughout our stay. Let`s just say that package was not for us, although it was destined to be great. The package we chose was absolutely amazing. Our package included transportation to the Magistrate where every couple had to submit the "original" divorce decree, if they were married before and fill out the application for marriage. We were interviewed by one of the counselors in a small office where a few questions were asked. Something that we did not know was that in the Bahamas, your original divorce decree is **kept.** Jason did not mind it, however, I am a paper hoarder, so of course, one of the first things I did upon returning home was to get a duplicate copy in case I needed it again.

Sandals Royal Bahamian Resort and Spa took care of all the important things. Sight seeing is on your own, however, only once did we manage time for that. Sandals gave a choice of having a minister or a Justice- of- the- Peace to perform the wedding ceremony which was also included in the package. Jason was so happy with how well everything unfolded that he bought one dozen roses for the wedding coordinator to show his appreciation for the little touches she added to our wonderful day.

Destination Weddings

When I began writing this book in 2004, our wedding was simply looked upon as a wedding in another country or an international wedding. During these past few years between 2004 and 2008 a new term has emerged for this type of wedding. The term is "destination weddings" meaning you go to another country or a state different from where you reside and get married.

The perspective bride and groom can now do a manual search or Google another country or this topic to find out what is offered when you go there to have your wedding. There are various groups, corporations and travel agents willing to assist you in your wedding location search and preparation. Some of the groups will assist you and be your wedding coordinator for a fee, to start.

There are very helpful free websites that can get you started asking the right questions and moving in the right direction regarding what you would like happen for that special day. They point out some of the helpful items found in this book and other tips.

Some of the most noted and popular destination wedding sites, (besides Las Vegas, Nevada) according to some of the literature I have read, are listed below:

1. Caribbean

2. Europe

3. Hawaii

4. Mexico

I also found that "theme weddings" are quite popular such as "Prince and Princess" or "Cinderella" weddings. The engaged couple that would like to have a luxurious wedding in a foreign country can also be accommodated by luxury wedding specialists who will do all of the planning for the happy couple and their guests. Some of these planners have a team of consultants, photographers, travel agents and others with the solitary purpose of facilitating your vision to completion. The team would also take care of all press releases regarding your wedding as part of the package. The only thing you would have to do is sit back, relax and show-up to the planned festivities.

CHAPTER 6
FINAL HAPPY THOUGHTS

There are many different wedding offers all over the world. They all have there own rules, regulations and international law requirements. If you want to do something different and very memorable for all who attend, then research where you might want to get married or renew your vows. Our family and our guests are still talking about their" invitation to a wedding in the Bahamas".

Keep in mind that you have to inform potential guests at least 6 months ahead of time so that they can work out reserving the time at work. One of the best things I like about our Bahamian wedding was that I could wear a very comfortable wedding gown, go bare-legged and where sandals.

Although not all marriages survive the test of time, the memory of this type of international wedding will "always" be beautiful. Whether you choose Mexico, Africa, Turks and Cacaos, Canada, Europe, Brazil or the Bahamas to name a few, make yours very special. If you live in the United States, you may want to get married in a country where your marriage certificate will be honored as legal in the United States. Possibly, one way to handle getting married where your marriage certificate is **not** recognized in the United States is to invite your minister or clergy to the wedding and let him/her participate in the ceremony also. This person may then give you a second marriage certificate when you return home, in addition to the one you receive from the country you are in.

Our wedding could not have been better for us and for our family and friends. The entire stay at Sandals was wonderful. The Resort`s staff told us that they also enjoyed our ceremony and reception because most brides and grooms only have their parents join them as witnesses to the wedding and to eat dinner afterwards. Our wedding ceremony with 3 brides-matrons and 1 matron-of-honor all dressed in a different shade of blue with the blue water behind them was a superior vision to behold and exceeded any thoughts we had imagined. The groomsmen, of course looked fantastic too.

I hope that sharing our wedding experience

makes you excited about the possibilities within your grasp. This book should hopefully ignite your enthusiasm to realize that you are able to have a great international wedding by just planning your desires and by researching for the location that best assists the expression of your passion. Enjoy wherever you go!

CHECKLIST FOR AN INTERNATIONAL WEDDING

o What time of year do you want to get married

o Choose 2 dates in case one is not available at your chosen location

o Research climate and conditions at your destination point

o Choose if you want to get married in an all inclusive or a-la-carte hotel/resort

o Call your selected destination and speak with the person who manages weddings at that organization so that you are certain to know what paper work you and the groom need

o Check your Passport to make sure it will still be current when you plan to leave or apply for a new Passport

o Start figuring out what attire you may want to get married in (e.g. full gown, short skirt, Tuxedo, Shorts, etc.)

o Write guest list of family and friends "you" could travel with and have around while on this special vacation

o Honeymoon plans completed

o Send a note, card or letter telling your invited guests to clear the date at least 6 months ahead of time, if possible, so that they can arrange that time off

o Order your invitations or find an invitation software program and personalize your invitations by making them

o Decide upon your favors and bridal party gifts

o Discuss with your groom if you would like to do something special, especially for both of your parents or other loved ones

o Discuss if you would like to invite or sponsor your clergy person to attend (keeping the marriage license in mind)

o If you use a travel agent, offer the agent to those who have indicated that they may attend o If you are unfamiliar with the quality of merchandise at your destination, it may be more practical to purchase favors or gifts prior to going to your international location

o Find out if there are entrance and/or exit fees for your location and make sure you save

o Check on how many days you and your groom have to reside in that country in order to marry there

o Send out your invitations 6 weeks prior to the wedding as a reminder for those who are attending

BIBLIOGRAPHY

1. DestinationWeddings.com;
   Retrieved 5/19/09:
   http://www.destinationweddings.com

2. Luxe Destination Weddings;
   Retrieved 5/20/09:
   http://www.luxedestinationweddings.com

3. Sandals Royal Bahamian Resort and Spa Brochure 2002; 2005